# WHAT IS A
# Fairy Tale?

ROBYN HARDYMAN

**Britannica**
Educational Publishing

IN ASSOCIATION WITH

**ROSEN**
EDUCATIONAL SERVICES

Published in 2014 by Britannica Educational Publishing (a trademark of Encyclopædia Britannica, Inc.) in association with The Rosen Publishing Group, Inc.
29 East 21st Street, New York, NY 10010

Distributed exclusively by Rosen Publishing.
To see additional Britannica Educational Publishing titles, go to rosenpublishing.com

First Edition

**<u>Britannica Educational Publishing</u>**
J.E. Luebering: Director, Core Reference Group
Anthony L. Green: Editor, Compton's by Britannica

**<u>Rosen Publishing</u>**
Hope Lourie Killcoyne: Executive Editor
Nelson Sá: Art Director

**Library of Congress Cataloging-in-Publication Data**

Hardyman, Robyn.
What is a Fairy Tale?/Robyn Hardyman. — First Edition.
    pages cm. — (The Britannica Common Core Library)
Includes bibliographical references and index.
ISBN 978-1-62275-215-7 (library binding) — ISBN 978-1-62275-218-8 (pbk.)_ISBN 978-1-62275-219-5 (6-pack)
1. Fairy tales. I. Title.
PN3437.H36 2014
398.2 — dc23
                                                                                2013022569

*Manufactured in the United States of America.*

**Photo credits**
Cover: Istockphoto: DaydreamsGirl bg, Sashkinw fg. Inside: Dreamstime: Chorazin3d 26, Crimsonrose 22, Egal 23, Pilotin 24, Yangx2 14–15; Istockphoto: Shutterstock: DaydreamsGirl 1bg, Sashkinw 1fg; Algol 28–29, Chungking 19, Agata Dorobek 5, Ellerslie 4, 11, 16–17, IgorGolovniov 6, Isoga 12, Kuco 8, 9, Oksana Merzlyakova 13, Noregt 6, One And Only 7, Silvionka 18, Boris Stroujko 11, Wongwean 21.

# CONTENTS

# What Is a Fairy Tale?

Fairy tales are stories written for children. They tell the story of a person having a difficult time, but they almost always have a happy ending. Fairy tales are full of wonderful characters, from evil witches and unicorns to fairies and elves. Storytellers based characters and settings for their fairy tales on places and people from their own culture.

Fairy tales often have magical settings and characters.

Fairy tales were first told aloud. They were passed down from one generation to another. As the stories were told over time, they changed. Eventually, fairy tales were written down. Since then, the stories have been rewritten many times.

**Generation** means people born at around the same time.

Most fairy tales were first told rather than written down, so their original authors are unknown.

# Why Are Fairy Tales Told?

Every culture has its own fairy tales that people tell to their children and pass down the generations. Fairy tales are told to entertain children and to also teach them the importance of characteristics such as love, kindness, and courage.

### STORYTELLERS

Hans Christian Andersen was a Danish storyteller. He wrote many great fairy tales, including *The Princess and the Pea* and *The Little Match Girl*.

*The Little Match Girl* is a story about a girl's dreams and hopes.

Many of the fairy tales we know today were collected and written down by two German brothers named Jakob and Wilhelm Grimm. They are better known as "the Brothers Grimm." The brothers wanted people everywhere to be able to read their stories. Fairy tales in their collection include *Rapunzel*, *The Frog Prince*, *Snow White*, and *Hansel and Gretel*.

**The Brothers Grimm**

# Themes in Fairy Tales

In fairy tales, good people struggle against difficulty caused by bad people. At the end of the tales, the good people win. Good characters in fairy tales often have luck or magic on their side.

The main characters in fairy tales are people. They can be children, kings and queens, or peasants. Fairy tales have **imaginary** characters, too, such as beasts, dwarfs, elves, fairy godmothers, witches, and giants.

**Imaginary** means not real, existing only in your imagination.

Snow White is helped by the seven dwarves.

Fairy tales are usually set in the past. The settings for fairy tales include castles, thick forests, and villages. Sometimes the settings are imaginary. In *Jack and the Beanstalk*, for example, the giant's home is at the top of an enormous magic beanstalk.

In *Sleeping Beauty,* a prince wakens the sleeping princess and breaks the wicked spell that sent her to sleep for 100 years.

# Fairy Tales Retold

Now that we know what fairy tales are and why they are told, let's read and **compare** some wonderful fairy tales from around the world.

## Cinderella

This fairy tale was first written down by a French author named Charles Perrault, in 1697.

*Cinderella lived with her stepmother and two mean stepsisters. One day, the prince invited the young ladies of the land to a ball. Cinderella longed to go, but her sisters would not let her. As Cinderella wept, her fairy godmother appeared. Using magic, the fairy godmother turned a pumpkin into a golden coach, mice into horses, and a rat into a coachman.*

**Compare** means to look at two or more things to see how alike or different they are.

*Cinderella's rags became a beautiful gown and a pair of glass slippers. The fairy godmother warned that the magic would end at midnight. At the ball, the prince and Cinderella fell in love. At midnight, she fled, leaving a slipper behind. The prince traveled the land to find the girl whose foot fit the slipper. Everyone tried it on. Eventually, Cinderella came forward. The prince had found his love, and they were married.*

Cinderella and her prince lived happily ever after in his fairy tale castle.

## Yeh-Shen

This fairy tale is from China.

Yeh-Shen lived with her stepmother and stepsister. Her stepmother was jealous of Yeh-Shen's beauty. Yeh-Shen's only friend was a fish with golden eyes. One day, her stepmother went to the lake and killed the fish. As Yeh-Shen's tears fell into the water, an old man appeared. He told her that the fish's bones were magic and would give Yeh-Shen all she wished for.

When the New Year festival came, the stepmother refused to let Yeh-Shen go. Yeh-Shen whispered to the bones that she wanted to go.

The bones of the fish with the golden eyes were magical.

Suddenly, she found herself dressed in a beautiful gown and slippers. At the **festival**, Yeh-Shen's stepsister saw her. Yeh-Shen ran away, leaving behind a slipper. A villager found the slipper. He sold it to a merchant, who gave it to the king. The king searched for the wearer of the slipper. When Yen-Shen tried it on, her beautiful dress returned. She and the king fell in love and were married.

A **festival** is a large public party held to celebrate something.

Yeh-Shen looked beautiful in her magical gown.

## Let's Compare

The characters and plots in *Cinderella* and *Yeh-Shen* are similar. Both have a young girl who is treated badly by a stepmother and stepsisters. Cinderella and Yeh-Shen are not allowed to go to a special event, but they are helped to get there by magic. As the girls run away, they lose a shoe.

In both stories, a slipper brings together the girls and their royal admirers.

The prince or king finds the shoe and searches for its wearer. Eventually he finds her, and they marry.

The setting of each story is different. In *Yeh-Shen*, it is typically Chinese, and the party is the **New Year festival**. In *Cinderella*, there is a dance at the royal castle. European princes lived in castles, and they gave balls.

The magic in Cinderella comes from a fairy godmother, instead of a fish.

The Chinese follow a different calendar from most other countries. There, the **New Year festival** takes place in February, when the new year starts.

# The Fisherman and His Wife
This story comes from Germany.

*A fisherman lived with his wife in a hut. One day, he caught a flounder fish.*

*"Please let me live," begged the fish. "I'm really a prince." The fisherman let him go. When he arrived home and told his wife, she scolded him.*

*"Why didn't you ask him for something? Ask him for a better house for us." So the fisherman did just that.*

*"Go home," said the fish. "You have a bigger house." It was true, but soon the wife was unhappy. She sent her husband to ask for a castle. They got their castle, but the wife told her husband she wanted to be queen.*

When her wish was granted, she demanded to be emperor. When that came true, she wanted to be pope.

Finally, the fisherman told the fish, "My wife wants to be like God."

"Go home," said the flounder. "She is back in her hut." And it was true.

> The fisherman's wife made her husband ask for more and more.

### The Stonecutter

This is a Japanese fairy tale.

*A stonecutter was at a rich man's house. He saw beautiful things and wished, "If only I had a bed with silk curtains, I would be happy!" A mountain spirit heard this and **granted** his wish. His house became a palace.*

**Granted** means to have given someone what they want.

The stonecutter's new bed curtains were made of beautiful Japanese silk.

One day, he saw a prince with a golden umbrella to protect him from the sun. He wished for this and it was granted to him. Still, the hot sun beat down. "I wish I were the sun!" he said. His wish was granted.

When a cloud hid the land from him and he wished to be a cloud, his wish was granted. For weeks he sent rain onto the land. It washed away everything except the rocks. "I wish I were a rock!" he said. The spirit granted his wish. When another stonecutter started working on the rock, he cried, "This child of Earth is more mighty than a rock! I wish I were a man!" The spirit granted his wish. Finally he was happy.

## Let's Compare

*The Fisherman and His Wife* and *The Stonecutter* are about being greedy. In the first story, the fisherman's wife wants to live in bigger and bigger houses. When she has that, she wants a more and more important title. When she asks to be like God, the fish punishes her for being too greedy.

The stonecutter wishes for greatness. Unlike the fisherman's wife, he finally realizes that what he had at the start of the tale was good enough. The lesson is that we must value what we have. We must not always long for more.

**STORYTELLERS**

*The Stonecutter* is also told in China. There is also a fairy tale in Russia with a very similar story.

The people that the fisherman's wife wishes to be—king, emperor, pope—were the most powerful men in Europe. The stonecutter wants to conquer nature instead.

Nature is often a powerful force in fairy tales.

## Jack and the Beanstalk

This fairy tale comes from England.

*A poor boy named Jack lived with his mother. One day, Jack sold their cow for some beans. His angry mother threw the beans out of the window.*

Jack's beans were magic, and they grew into an enormous beanstalk that climbed up into the clouds.

The next morning, an enormous beanstalk had grown. Jack climbed it, and at the top, he found a house, where a woman lived. She told Jack to hide, because her husband was a giant who ate boys.

The giant came in and boomed, "Fee, fie, fo, fum, I smell the blood of an Englishman! Be he alive or be he dead, I'll grind his bones to make my bread!"

Jack escaped with a bag of gold. Later, he returned and stole a hen that laid golden eggs. The third time, he stole a golden harp. As he was escaping, the harp cried, "Master!" The giant heard it and chased Jack down the beanstalk. Quickly, Jack chopped down the beanstalk. The giant died and Jack and his mother were rich and happy.

## Thirteenth

This is a story from Italy about the youngest boy of thirteen brothers.

*There was once a terrible ogre, so the king promised gold to anyone who stole the ogre's blanket. Thirteenth's mean brothers said he would do it. They all hoped the ogre would hurt him.*

*Thirteenth went to the ogre's house, and hid. The ogre called, "I smell the smell of human flesh! Where I see it, I will swallow it!" Thirteenth stole the blanket and ran away.*

*The king then offered gold for the ogre's horse. Thirteenth stole it. Next, the king wanted the ogre's pillow.*

**STORYTELLERS**

*Thirteenth* was first published by an American writer named Thomas Frederick Crane, in 1885.

*This had bells on it, so it made a noise when Thirteenth snatched it. The ogre grabbed Thirteenth, and put him in a barrel, but he escaped.*

*Then the king sent Thirteenth to fetch the ogre. Thirteenth took a huge chest with him and tricked the ogre into climbing inside. He returned the barrel to the king. The ogre was kept in chains for the rest of his life. The king gave Thirteenth all the riches he could wish for.*

Thirteenth captured the ogre in a huge chest, and took him back to the king.

## Let's Compare

The plots and the characters of *Jack and the Beanstalk* and *Thirteenth* are very similar. A boy uses his cleverness to steal precious things from an ogre. The boy finally kills or captures the ogre himself, and becomes rich.

Ogres often appear in fairy tales. They are scary, wicked characters that have to be defeated.

The settings of both stories are also similar. The ogres live in huge houses. But there is less magic in *Thirteenth*. There is no beanstalk, or hen that lays golden eggs, or talking harp. Thirteenth steals ordinary things, and uses his own smart thinking.

In both stories the "hero" tricks the giant. Jack kills him by chopping down the beanstalk. Thirteenth gives the ogre to the king, who makes him live in chains. These are not good ways to behave, but the boys become rich. Some versions of the stories explain how the ogres were very bad. They stole from the people, and killed them. In these stories, the boys act more **justly**.

**Justly** means acting fairly.

# Write Your Own Fairy Tale

Are you ready to write your own fairy tale? Here are some simple steps to help you start:

**1. Pick your setting:** Do you want a modern location, or do you like tales set in castles and forests?

**2. Think of a plot:** It must include a struggle between good and bad, and a message about good ways to behave. It can also include some magic.

Let your imagination run wild to create a magical tale!

**3. Find your characters:** They can be modern, or from long ago. They can even be imaginary and magical, such as elves and fairy godmothers! Choose some good characters and some bad ones.

**4. Sketch your fairy tale:** Make a "map" of the story showing the start, middle, and end.

**5. Write and rewrite!** Write your fairy tale, then read it through and change anything you do not like.

Finished? Read your fairy tale to a friend or a family member. Send it in an e-mail to your teacher, your family, and your friends. You could even post it onto your family's website or blog.

# GLOSSARY

**ball** A dance.

**characteristics** A person's good and bad qualities.

**characters** Those featured in a story. In fairy tales the characters can be people or magical beings, such as elves and fairy godmothers.

**coachman** The man responsible for driving a horse-drawn coach.

**courage** Bravery.

**culture** The customs and traditions of a group of people.

**defeated** Beaten.

**elves** Small imaginary creatures with magical powers.

**emperor** The ruler of an empire.

**fairy godmothers** Imaginary fairies with magical powers who advise and help people as a parent would.

**greedy** Wanting more than you really need.

**harp** A stringed musical instrument.

**location** The place where a story happens.

**merchant** A person who buys and sells things for a living.

**ogre** An imaginary evil giant.

**peasants** Poor people.

**plots** Events that happen in a story, such as a fairy tale.

**pope** The head of the Roman Catholic Church.

**royal** To do with a king, queen, or member of their family.

**scolded** Shouted at.

**settings** Where stories takes place.

**spirit** A magical, invisible being.

**stepmother** A woman married to a person's father who is not the person's mother.

**stepsisters** Daughters of a stepmother or stepfather.

**stonecutter** Someone who cuts and carves stones.

**unicorns** Magical, horselike creatures with wings and a horn on their heads.

**versions** Different stories about the same thing, but with different details.

## Books

Andersen, Hans Christian. *Tales of Hans Christian Andersen*. Somerville, MA: Candlewick Press, 2010.

Hoberman, Mary Ann. *You Read to Me, I'll Read to You: Very Short Fairy Tales to Read Together*. New York, NY: Little, Brown Books, 2012.

Hoffman, Mary. *A First Book of Fairy Tales*. London, UK: Dorling Kindersley, 2006.

Loewen, Nancy. *Once Upon a Time: Writing Your Own Fairy Tale*. North Mankato, MN: Picture Window Books, 2009.

Somaiah, Rosemarie. *Indian Children's Favorite Stories*. North Clarendon, VT: Tuttle Publishing, 2006.

## Websites

Due to the changing nature of Internet links, Rosen Publishing has developed an online list of Websites related to the subject of this book. This site is updated regularly. Please use this link to access the list:

http://www.rosenlinks.com/corel/fairy